Thomas Jefferson

by Simone T. Ribke

Content Consultant

Nanci R. Vargus, Ed.D.
Professor Emeritus, University of Indianapolis

Reading Consultant

Jeanne Clidas, Ph.D.
Reading Specialist

Children's Press®
An Imprint of Scholastic Inc.
New York Toronto London Auckland Sydney
Mexico City New Delhi Hong Kong
Danbury, Connecticut

Library of Congress Cataloging-in-Publication Data
Ribke, Simone T.
 Thomas Jefferson/by Simone T. Ribke; poem by Jodie Shepherd.
     pages cm. — (Rookie biographies)
 Includes bibliographical references and index.
 Audience: Ages 3-6.
ISBN 978-0-531-20560-0 (library binding: alk. paper) — ISBN 978-0-531-21203-5 (pbk.: alk. paper)
  1. Jefferson, Thomas, 1743-1826—Juvenile literature. 2. Presidents—United States—Biography—
Juvenile literature. I. Shepherd, Jodie. II. Title.

 E332.79.R53 2014
 973.4'6092—dc23 [B]   2014015030

No part of this publication may be reproduced in whole or in part, or stored in a retrieval
system, or transmitted in any form or by any means, electronic, mechanical, photocopying,
recording, or otherwise, without written permission of the publisher. For information regarding
permission, write to Scholastic Inc., Attention: Permissions Department,
557 Broadway, New York, NY 10012.

Produced by Spooky Cheetah Press
Poem by Jodie Shepherd
Design by Keith Plechaty

© 2015 by Scholastic Inc.

All rights reserved. Published in 2015 by Children's Press, an imprint of Scholastic Inc.

Printed in China 62

SCHOLASTIC, CHILDREN'S PRESS, ROOKIE BIOGRAPHIES®, and associated logos are
trademarks and/or registered trademarks of Scholastic Inc.

7 8 9 10 R 24 23 22 21 20 19

Photographs ©: Alamy Images: 4, 30 right (Everett Collection Inc), 8, 24 (North Wind Picture
Archives); AP Images/North Wind Picture Archives: 12, 31 center top; Bridgeman Art Library/
Peter Newark American Pictures: 27; Library of Congress: 15; Media Bakery/Chris Parker: 11;
Shutterstock, Inc.: 28, 31 center bottom (Cvandyke), 3 bottom (Mesut Dogan), cover (Rick
Grainger); Superstock, Inc.: 16 (Chris Parker/Axiom Photographic), 20, 23, 31 bottom; The Granger
Collection: 19; Thinkstock: 3 top right (Daniel R. Burch), 3 top left, 30 left (Kyle McMahon).

Maps by XNR Productions, Inc.

Scholastic Inc., 557 Broadway, New York, NY 10012.

Table of Contents

Meet Thomas Jefferson

Thomas Jefferson was one of the "Founding Fathers" of the United States. He helped write the Declaration of Independence. He helped shape the first laws of our nation. He was the country's third **President**.

Jefferson was born on April 13, 1743. His family lived in Virginia on a plantation, which is a very large farm.

Back then, Virginia was an English **colony**. America was not a country. It was made up of 13 colonies that were ruled by the King of England.

Thomas was born in Virginia.

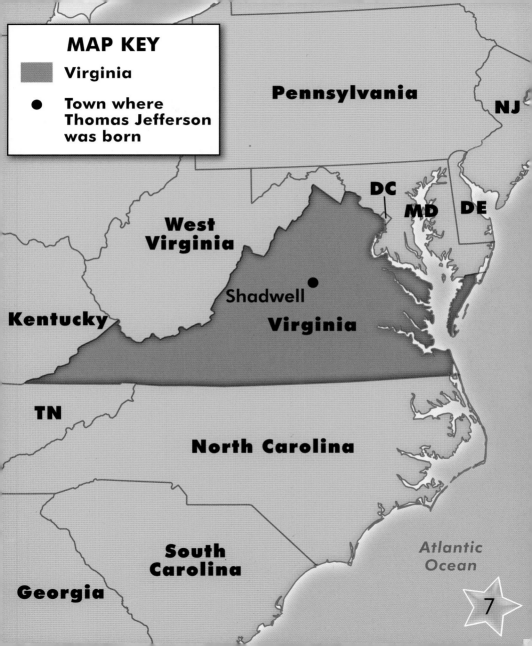

MAP KEY

Virginia

● Town where Thomas Jefferson was born

Pennsylvania

NJ

West Virginia

DC

MD

DE

Kentucky

Shadwell

Virginia

TN

North Carolina

South Carolina

Georgia

Atlantic Ocean

Jefferson came from a rich family. He was a good student and a great writer. He was 16 when he started college. Jefferson studied how to help others understand the law. He became a lawyer.

People can still visit Monticello today.

Jefferson began building his famous home when he was 26. He called this plantation Monticello.

Soon after, Jefferson married Martha Wayles Skelton. They had six children.

FAST FACT!

Jefferson was an inventor. He invented many useful items. One was a plow that made farming easier.

Freedom Writer

In 1775, Americans began to fight for **independence**. They did not want to be ruled by the King of England. Many felt that the King's laws were unfair.

FAST FACT!

The American Revolution is also known as the War of Independence. It lasted eight years, from 1775 to 1783.

In 1776, Jefferson wrote the Declaration of Independence. This important paper told the King that he could not rule the Americans anymore. But the Americans would not truly be free until they won the war. In 1783, America became a new country called the United States.

Jefferson works on the Declaration of Independence with Benjamin Franklin (left) and John Adams (center).

Rising Star

In 1779, Jefferson became the governor of Virginia. He wrote a law that gave people in Virginia freedom of religion. Unlike the people in England, those in America would be able to practice any religion.

Jefferson helped to start the University of Virginia.

In 1785, American leaders asked Jefferson to do an important job for the new government. Jefferson became the representative to France. He helped the United States and French governments learn about each other. It was hoped that France would become a good friend to our new nation.

FAST FACT!

Jefferson had many books. He sold them to the government to help start the Library of Congress.

In 1796, Jefferson ran to become the second President of the United States. He lost by three votes. John Adams became the President. Jefferson became the Vice President.

John Adams was America's second President.

President Jefferson

In 1800, Jefferson ran for President again. This time, the vote was a tie. Another vote had to be held to decide. Jefferson was the winner! He became America's third President.

This map shows how much land was added to America through the Louisiana Purchase.

Jefferson was President for eight years. During that time, he did many important things. He bought land from France. This land was called the Louisiana Territory. It made the United States twice as big as before!

Americans did not know much about the new land in the west. President Jefferson hired two men to explore the area. Their names were Meriwether Lewis and William Clark. Their trip helped Americans learn a lot about this new land.

FAST FACT!

An American Indian woman named Sacagawea was an important part of Lewis and Clark's team. She saved their lives many times.

Timeline of Thomas Jefferson's Life

1770
begins to build Monticello

1743
born on April 13

1772
marries Martha Wayles Skelton

President Jefferson died on July 4, 1826. A **monument** was built to honor him. It is called the Jefferson Memorial. When people visit the memorial, they remember how President Jefferson worked to make America the free and fair country that it is today.

1776
writes the Declaration of Independence

1803
buys the Louisiana Territory; sends Lewis and Clark to explore the west

1797
becomes Vice President

1801
becomes President

1826
dies on July 4

A Poem About Thomas Jefferson

Jefferson's life deserves celebration—
farmer, inventor, President of our nation.
He wrote the Declaration of Independence, too.
It's amazing what one single person can do.

You Can Make a Difference

If you see something that is unfair, you can work to change it. Like Jefferson, you can use words to make a difference. Write a letter to someone in power who might be able to help you.

Glossary

colony (KOL-uh-nee): a place that is settled by people from another country

independence (in-di-PEN-duhns): freedom from being ruled by others

monument (MON-yuh-muhnt): a building or statue that is built to remember someone or something important

president (PREZ-uh-duhnt): the elected leader of a country

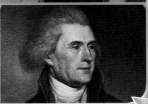

Index

Facts for Now

Visit this Scholastic Web site for more information on Thomas Jefferson:

www.factsfornow.scholastic.com

Enter the keywords **Thomas Jefferson**

About the Author

Simone T. Ribke writes children's books and educational materials. She lives with her family in Maryland.